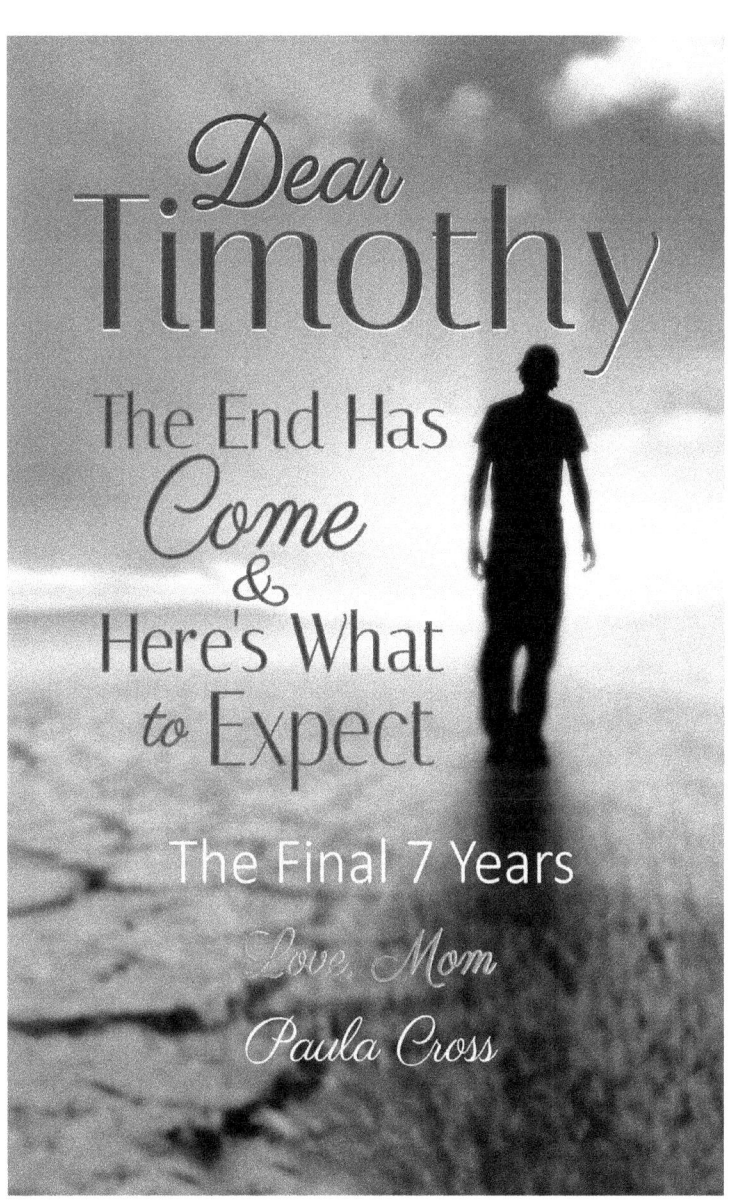

Copyright © 2023 by Paula Cross

All rights reserved.

No portion of this book may be reproduced without written permission from the publisher or author, except as permitted by U.S. copyright law. For bulk orders may be purchased through the Church Members Center at Ldwcfamily.com.

Though presented as a letter to the author's son, this publication is intended to provide accurate and authoritative information in regard to Biblical End Times Prophecy.

While the publisher and the author have used due diligence and best efforts to prepare this book, they make no representations or warranties with respect to the accuracy or completeness of the contents of its contents. Readers must weigh, discern, and prayerfully consider its contents for themselves, and are responsible for their own conclusions.

Book Cover by Paula Cross. Cover background image by kwest19 at Canstockphoto.com.

Siebert Publishing, LLC, Pittsburgh PA 15235

Published September 2023

TeachingVideos:
https://www.youtube.com/@LastDaysWitness

Church: Lastdayswitnesschurch.org

Church Members Community Center: Ldwcfamily.com

ISBN: 978-0-9991646-6-2

Table of Contents

Ch. 1: Salutation ----------------------------- Pg 9

Ch. 2: Is It Really the End? ------------------- Pg 15

Ch. 3: The Final Seven Year Summary --------- Pg 23

Ch. 4: The Final Feasts of the Lord ----------- Pg 47

Ch. 5: The Rise of the Beast ------------------ Pg 69

Ch. 6: Many Won't Believe It's the End -------- Pg 79

Ch. 7: The Tribulations Are Necessary --------- Pg 85

Ch. 8: What to Do & How to Be Safe ---------- Pg 99

Chapter One

Salutation

Dear Timothy,

I know you're aware that something disturbing is going on in the world. That even despite your recent rebellion against the Creator, you know full well... something's up. That life as we know it has gone off the deep end, and everything is about to come to a head. In fact, I bet despite the distance between us, you'd agree with me that it doesn't take rocket science to discern that the world is quickly spinning out of control.

Well, it's all because time is about up. And what do I mean by that? I'm going to explain it all to you in this letter. And you need to listen to every word. Doing so will be the difference between life and death and, even more pressing, eternal torment versus eternity in paradise. Whether you want to hear this or not, you absolutely must. Everyone must. I assure you, you will watch everything I tell you unfold right before your eyes over the next few years.

And how do I know what I am talking about? I have spent the last seven years deeply studying the scriptures concerning the end times. God laid it all out in the Bible. It's difficult to see off the cuff. You have to search all of the scriptures and piece the puzzle together. It is phenomenal how all the pieces were from different authors over the course of hundreds and even thousands of years. You have to sincerely seek and study by the power of the Holy Spirit. I still haven't discovered all there is to know. Nowhere close. But I've come to see a lot over the years. Honestly, I thought I had it all figured out seven years ago and I've been longing to tell you what I know ever since then. But the time wasn't right, so I held my tongue. Then, over the years, as I discovered more and more pieces of the puzzle throughout scripture, I understood that there was still much to learn. And then as things unfolded in the world, I began connecting many dots. Today, though I don't know everything, I've come to understand the overall picture of what the final seven years look like. And I'm called to warn as many people as I can.

So the moment I've been waiting for, to tell you everything, has arrived. I am desperate for you to be fully aware of the truth so that you aren't destroyed along with the rest of the world. I beg of you to hear me out.

Don't worry, I know you're not very familiar with scripture so I'm going to explain everything as basic as possible. I will include scripture references in case you want to look things up for yourself which would be awesome. But, like I said, I'm just going to lay out the overarching picture point by point so that you understand what's going on and what to do.

The bottom line is the end is beginning. We are currently, or very, very soon to enter, the final seven years of life as we know it prior to Jesus coming down to the earth to reign. What I tell you in this letter is the purest truth you'll likely come across concerning the day and hour we've entered. There are many voices out there speaking to this topic and they will not agree with what I tell you. Understand that there is an enemy hard at work to keep people, especially followers of Christ, confused and asleep. So the powers and principalities of darkness have gone to great lengths to saturate the media, using all sorts of voices, including scholars and their teachings and books, mainstream church preachers, and even obscure folks on social media or youtube to pollute, twist, waterdown, and distort the truth of the times. There are hundreds of different perspectives and ideas as to what's what. Especially pertaining to the interpretation of the last days' timetable laid out in the Bible. The devil is behind it all. He knew he had to work diligently to saturate the earth with all sorts of conflicting teachings and nonsense.

So who should you or anyone else believe? How do you know who's telling the truth? Well, you must be very, very careful about everything you hear! Deception is extremely high! You must always ask the Lord, **"In the Name of Jesus Christ, the Son of God who came in the flesh, is this true or false?"**, when you listen to anyone teach about faith or the Bible. Make sure you pray as I just said, otherwise lying spirits will say yes when you ask if something is false. So always pray in that very way, asking with a sincere desire, if the teachers or teachings are of the Holy, Living God, or not. Even pray this way concerning me! Beyond that, you'll see who is telling the truth when what they tell you, in conjunction with it also lining up with scripture, of course, unfolds right before your eyes.

I am praying that you will see reality, not the illusions of the enemy. I have, and continue to pray, that all deceptions in your soul, mind, heart, and spirit are broken off of you. I broke their power in the Name and by the authority of the one and only true Jesus Christ of Nazareth. And I pray the SAME for anyone else who reads this letter who belongs to Jesus. Amen. So, you will see the truth, the whole truth, and nothing but the truth. Unfortunately, most who think they're Christians because that's what their family said they were, or for whatever reason other than truly seeking Jesus with all their hearts, won't realize or believe it's the final seven years. But the way to know that it actually is, is to see if what I'm saying is true by watching it unfold.

And don't worry, I'm not only going to tell you exactly what to expect, I'll also let you know how to be safe, guiding you as to what you need to do. And then... I am going to share this letter with the world. I can only hope that you will do the same.

Like I said, I want to keep this simple. But the biggest question everyone has is when the rapture will occur. I have written a book that proves why the rapture is in the middle of the seven year tribulation period. It actually debunks the false teachings of a pre-trib, post-trib, and pre-wrath rapture. So I won't explain why the rapture is in the middle of the seven years here. But anyway, that book is written for scholars who are quite familiar with scripture, so it's a bit complex. Meanwhile, I'm working on all kinds of teachings on my youtube channel which also speak a great deal as to why the rapture happens mid trib. But like I said, I'm writing you this overview of the entire timeline without all the details broken down. I just want to give you solid insight as to what's going to happen so you will know what to do.

Is It Really The End?

Before I explain what's happening, I need to demonstrate how we can know for sure that *it really is the end* of life as we know it, that Jesus is definitely coming back very, very soon. As in, by the end of this decade. And if I'm wrong, then within just a year or two thereafter. Because everything that needs to be in place... pretty much is.

There are many things that the Bible says will occur before, or, in order for, Jesus to return to earth. After he left nearly 2000 years ago, and Jerusalem was destroyed in 70 A. D., which caused the nation of Israel to cease to exist, scattering surviving Jews all over the world, it has been impossible for the Lord to return.

One interesting and amazing prophecy that shows God's hand in everything, is not only that Israel is a nation again, but that it's now one of the most plentiful nations in the world. This is profound because Israel has always been 60% desert wilderness and rock. And after 70 A.D., even as other nations made it their home, it wasn't all that fertile and productive. But Isaiah 41:18-20 tells us that God would make His land lush with water and greenery, and concludes the prophecy by saying, "That they may see and know, and consider and understand together, that the hand of the Lord has done this.". And as of today, ever since Israel became a nation again in 1948, the land has become insanely plentiful and lush, just as Isaiah prophesied.

And that leads to my next point. In Matthew 24, Mark 13, and Luke 21, it discusses how the disciples asked Jesus what would be the sign of the end and His coming. His answer included, *"When you see the abomination of desolation in the temple and Jerusalem surrounded, those in Judea, meaning Jerusalem, had better flee!"* But if Jerusalem and the temple were destroyed forty years later in 70 A.D., after Jesus had said that, which scattered the Jews and meant Israel was no longer a nation, how could Jesus warn about an invasion of Jerusalem before His coming? Except that Israel would have to become a nation again. And there'd have to be another temple built!

So for 1,878 years after Israel was scattered, it was totally impossible for Jesus to return. But the day Israel became a nation again, which was completely amazing in and of itself, it became possible for Jesus to come back. But there were other prophecies that also needed to be in place first, as well. Such as Isaiah 41's depiction of the astonishing lush greenery of the land that had never been possible in ancient times.

Then Daniel 12:4 says, *"But you, Daniel, shut up the words, and seal the book until the time of the end; when many shall run to and fro, and knowledge shall increase."* If that's not a crystal clear depiction of our world today, I don't know what is!

And Revelation 11:9 says, *"Then those from the **peoples, tribes, tongues, and nations** will see their dead bodies 3 1/2 days, and not allow their dead bodies to be put into graves."* This refers to the two witnesses who will be killed by the antichrist in Jerusalem. But how can all the nations of the world see images of these two dead bodies in real time, except that this prophecy must transpire during a time when global communication existed? Up until a couple decades ago when everyone started having world-wide internet access, this was an impossibility.

Zechariah 14:12 says, *"And this shall be the plague with which the Lord will strike all the people who fought against Jerusalem: Their flesh shall dissolve while they stand on their feet, their eyes shall dissolve in their sockets, and their tongues shall dissolve in their mouths.".* This is clearly weaponry that sounds like nuclear bombs or something like it, which we all know never existed until recent times.

As for the mark of the beast, that's a sign of the times in and of itself, because global currency was always an impossibility until now, with all the global communication and technologies in place.

Along these same lines, we know that in order for the antichrist to become a global leader, the nations must be primed for this. This is what the whole point of the United Nations has been all along. I mean, think about it. There are hundreds of individualized countries who make up their own rules and stand completely independent of every other nation. Rulers of nations love having their own power over a people or territory. But little by little, many of them have been unknowingly laying down their individuality. Never in history that I know of has a nation said, *"Hey, let's all join together and be one big happy family, give up our individual powers and let one person be in charge of all of us!"* Really? No way! Yet, that's what's been happening in slow motion. They don't even recognize it. Between the UN and the one world religion set into motion in September 2022, world powers have been becoming a single entity for quite some time. But, in order for a full-on unity where they all come under a single leader to ever happen, utter chaos will have to hit the planet. And that's precisely what's about to happen.

So clearly, the world looks exactly how the Bible describes things to be at the time of Christ's return. People from just one hundred years ago had had none of this in place. It was totally impossible for Jesus to come back then - or even 30 years ago. I can't imagine that a one world currency would have been possible even 10 years ago! But now, oh yes, it's perfectly doable!

And here's something interesting. Though there's no emphasis on timing concerning this, it's astonishing that the Dead Sea, which never had fish living in it, suddenly does! And then there's the Euphrates River which, despite being 1,740 miles long, according to Revelation 16:12, it will dry up in order for the kings of the east to travel on foot to the battle of Armageddon. And this has already begun! Reports of the Euphrates River drying up have been in the news for a while now!

On top of all this, we can see how things are pointing to the imminent start of World War III. This is so very much at the door. And based on the Bible's warning that Israel will be invaded and Mystery Babylon the Great will be destroyed in one hour, and then later God destroying the nations that invade Israel, this tells me that World War III takes place in the second half of the seven year tribulation period.

But there is still one more major requirement that needs to happen before Jesus can come back.

Though some people say this is not the case, I'm convinced that since the Bible reflects upon there being a temple in Matthew 24 and Revelation 11, in discussions concerning the time of Christ's return, then this is definitely a prerequisite.

I already mentioned how the third temple in Jerusalem is soon to be built. But how soon? It's well known that the Jews have everything ready to begin building. Levitical priests have been trained and ordained. Supplies, materials and sacred elements have been produced and are lined up. And they finally have three red heifers on deck, of which at least one needs to remain spotless to qualify to serve as the required sacrifice in order to build the temple. Some people are disappointed that these spotless, solid red heifers which can't grow even a single black hair, are a product of man's manipulation, not a natural miracle. But what they need to realize is God didn't personally authorize the construction of this third temple because, when Jesus died for the sins of the world, the Jewish temple was no longer necessary for Him as a medium between God and man. Moreover, He said man is now His temple, where His Spirit lives. So, God would have never provided a perfect red heifer. Man had to make it happen. And it looks like they have it. They had five one year old perfect red heifers in September of 2022. Since then, as of summer 2023, two of them have been disqualified. And now there's only a couple months remaining before they are of the right age to be sacrificed.

So, as far as I'm aware, this means unless all three of these red heifers grow black hairs in the next couple of months, EVERYTHING is in place for this temple to be built! And the only thing preventing them from starting to build as early as the fall of 2023, is the issue concerning the temple mount. An agreement, such as a two-state solution, will need to be made so that this temple can be built peacefully. Though this two state solution is likely how the Jews will finally be able to build the temple, the problem is Jerusalem is GOD'S LAND. And their agreeing to divide it is a violation to the very God they're supposedly building the temple for. And this, along with their adherence to the false Messiah, the antichrist, is what sets the great and terrible Day of the Lord and Israel's invasion... into motion! The final straw, though, is when the antichrist sets himself up as God in this temple. Very, very soon after this is when the Great Tribulation begins.

All this to prove, there's no doubt about it. Jesus can definitely come back now. The only other thing that needs to happen... is this seven years of tribulation. Which is likely to begin between 2023 and 2024, most likely in conjunction with the two state solution, or on account of some other covenant that's confirmed with many, according to Daniel 9:27.

And what's the one final factor which proves that we can be absolutely certain of all this?

Based on the 6000 years of recorded Biblical history that will be ending by or around the year 2030, we know the seventh thousand years will begin. And on day one of the seventh thousand years, the Bible says Jesus will be on the earth reigning and ruling as King. So, what more can be said? The end is surely upon us.

Chapter Three

The Final Seven Year Summary

FIRST - HERE'S A SUPER CONDENSED SUMMATION

2023-2030 Projection

Anywhere from <u>Sept 2023 to Sept 2024</u>, depending on when the Covenant w/ Many occurs, the Final 7 Yr Countdown Will Begin, and We'll See:

Ever-increasing Disasters, Major Earthquake splits USA, Economic Shock, Resources & Food Shortages, Great Global Famine / Plague, which will likely peak in 2026, killing hundreds of millions, Antichrist identity will become apparent, and there'll be a significant rise in UFO sightings.

From <u>Sept 2026 to March 2027</u> (or 2028 depending on when the covenant was made) In the Midst of the Seven Years, We'll See:

Aliens/UFOs common, Mega global persecution against the true church activists, the Abomination of Desolation, The Big Lie / False Messiah / Aliens, Sun/Moon darkened / Asteroid strikes the earth / 5 Month Torment of the non-sealed begins as the 2 Witnesses are killed, WWIII /sky opens & Jesus is seen in sky, Earthquake in Jerusalem / Rapture of the Blameless, the Mark of Beast becomes global law.

<u>2031</u> - The New Jerusalem / Tabernacles w/ Christ

Despite what anyone says, the Bible clearly shows a series of events that will occur before Jesus returns, which do fit into a seven year timeframe. And these seven years are divided into two parts. The first half consists of 3 ½ years of birthing pangs, or "the beginnings of sorrows", as Jesus called them. According to Matthew 24 and elsewhere, this first half contains increasing disasters, wars, rumors of wars, famine, lawlessness, and the most severe, global persecution ever, against the true Christians by the corporate body of Christ, yes, by the main Christian church system. And then a final indicator that the Great Tribulation, or the second half, is about to begin, is that the gospel of the kingdom of God will be preached in power, with great miracles, to all nations, just as Jesus had done before He was crucified.

Note that for 2000 years since Jesus was here the first time, there have been many miracles and healings. But during the first half of the tribulation, the world will begin to see an ever-increasing level of God's glory and miracles like never before. Especially as the middle of the seven years approaches. This is because God will anoint many believers with His Spirit and power during this time, in order to demonstrate that He is a mighty God. Many will refer to this as the Great Glory Revival, the greatest ever. This outpouring of God's glory will bring in a great harvest of souls just before Jesus comes to gather us in the middle of the seven years. And there will be two specific witnesses in Jerusalem prophesying and preaching in power to the Jews, calling them to faith in Jesus Christ before the great and terrible Day of the Lord begins.

Simultaneous to the mighty move of God and His glory sweeping across particular regions, the dark kingdom will be putting on his supernatural show to compete with people's attention and to divert them away from the truth, and God's glory. The enemy will perform his own signs and wonders to deceive the masses. And the Bible tells us that before the people of God are raptured, it will be like the days of Noah, yes, in that people will be living their lives as normal, having no clue what's about to hit them, but I believe it will also be like how there were giants and angel-human cross breeds, or hybrids, saturating the earth in the times of Noah - which was the whole reason for the flood! In fact, these hybrids supposedly already walk the earth as spawn of the grays mixed with human DNA, according to sources like L.A. Marzulli and people's eye witness accounts. On top of this, some people have prophesied that aliens and UFOs will be on the news more and more frequently, beginning in 2025 onward, with it all becoming "normal". In fact, it is strongly suspected that the current rise in UFO sightings and all the eerie, unexplainable sounds in the skies, serve to pave the way for this particular deception to take hold of humanity as legitimate, which will all connect, somehow, to the rise of antichrist. Some believers have even prophesied that the antichrist will claim that the rapture of the believers isn't actually a rapture of Christ, but was a measure taken by these "supreme beings", to punish the trouble-making Christians. And that antichrist will quite possibly take credit for ridding these people from the earth, as well.

By the way, as for the devout servants of the Lord who walk in great miracles during the first half of the seven years, who cast out demons and preach against the great apostasy, which is currently underway, I want to tell you that they are called watchmen. In the scriptures, such as Ezekiel 33:3-9, watchmen are required to warn people of God's impending punishment, or they, themselves, will be in trouble with God. This is because, though God is angry with His rebellious children and must discipline them to bring them into repentance, this proves He goes to such extreme measures, requiring the believers who love Him with all their hearts, to be fully submitted to His sufferings, even unto death, in order to warn and save people. God requires them to sound the alarms that the end is upon us so that nobody can say God didn't warn them and give them every opportunity to get right, before taking them to the woodshed. God loves everyone so much that He's willing to ask His bondservants to be willing to die for this cause! And, since the bondservants, or watchmen, know that the middle of the seven years is when the Great Tribulation begins, they must use these precious last few hours to warn as many as possible, with all they have in them, and call them all to repentance. No matter the cost. *Or they're in big trouble with God, themselves.*

Meanwhile, everyone who listens to the warnings and repents, and truly renounces sin, will be made clean so that when Jesus descends in the clouds in the middle of the seven years to gather His spotless people, these are the ones who will be taken up to Heaven. You can see this in 1 Thessalonians 4:15-17, and 1 Corinthians 15:51-52.

The reason Jesus will come to get all the spotless, repentant believers, is because He is about to pour out His anger on the earth at this time to discipline all of His people who continue to bow to false gods, and still refuse to repent. You might think that God pours out His wrath on random people during the entire 3 1/2 years of Great Tribulation. But this is not so. No. His focus is on His disobedient children and the Jews who continue to reject Him and now have agreed to divide His land and show homage to the false Messiah! So, instead of destroying all of the wicked, Jesus first lashes out in fury on the Jews - both the native, old covenant Jews, as well as the new covenant adulterous Christians, Babylonian Jews of Revelation 17! The Bible says judgment begins at the house of God in 1 Peter 4:17. So the Great Tribulation will begin with an invasion on Jerusalem, and potentially, upon the USA because

America is a daughter nation of God, and Mystery Babylon the Great, the scarlet whore of Revelation who rides the beast, as well.

At about the same time that these invasions occur is when God's servants and all who repented and are spotless, will be raptured. Because the Bible says His children are not appointed to wrath. You can see this in 1 Thessalonians 5:9. And after the rapture takes place is when all hell will break loose on earth like never before.

Jesus said the Great Tribulation will be worse than anything ever in history. And there've been some horrible times. World War I killed 20 million people and wounded about another 20 million. World War II killed a total of around 53 million people. And when we think of the Holocaust which killed 6 million Jews, the sheer cruelty of how they murdered these innocent people is absolutely insane! Yet, Jesus said the Great Tribulation will be worse than all of that!

Just before the Great Tribulation starts, Revelation 9 tells us about an unleashing of demons from the bottomless pit, as well as four other demonic angels who have been bound in the River Euphrates being released - all to wreak havoc on the world. These demonic powers may just possess the hybrids and supernaturally empower them. The scripture tells us they will have the power to torment those who do not have the seal of God on their foreheads for five months. This means the ones who ARE tormented for five months are the Christians who are living in sin or who are in apostasy with the scarlet whore - because these believers do not have the seal of God on their foreheads, which includes protection.

Meanwhile, another portion of Revelation 9 says that one of the beasts that comes from the pit will possess the eloquent man who seems to have all the answers, who had just come into position as the one world leader! In fact, the Bible says he will suffer a fatal wound but will miraculously come back to life, and that all the world will marvel over him! Yet, as soon as he's in charge, he sets the mark of the beast into effect, where everyone is forced to take his mark in the hand or forehead, or else they cannot buy, sell, or trade! People who don't want the mark will have to go into hiding and live their lives constantly fleeing the relentless beast! While people who do take the mark go on living hunky dory for a while, they end up in utter agony a few years later and ultimately, are cast into the eternal Lake of Fire!

And while all this torment is going on, on top of the increasing natural disasters, lack of resources, nuclear wars, severe oppression from the antichrist, demon hybrids everywhere, people eating people, the Word of God being illegal, His lack of presence and peace, the increasing heat and even freezing winters, and all else, the Bible says ⅓ of mankind will be killed by the war. That's about 2.5 billion people!

So to recap, though full of natural disasters, great plague, and horrendous famine, the first 3 ½ years is a time of warning by the true servants, or watchmen, calling the world to repent. There will be miracles going on everywhere including healing, body parts being replaced, the dead being raised, blind eyes being opened, and so on. Though the corporate church system and its one world religion agenda will be perturbed with the true servants, eventually having laws made to imprison and even kill them, the true people of God will continue to be a bright light in very dark places, to whom many will run. And these servants of God will be untouchable, having supernatural protection from God until their job to warn is finished. Disaster might be all around them but not a hair on their heads will be harmed. Instead, they'll be there to help the devastated, hurting people. Healing them and even raising up their loved ones from the dead, and bringing them into the saving knowledge of Christ. Jesus will go to great lengths through His servants at this time to save the lost and to prove His love and the validity of His kingdom. People will finally realize there is an Almighty God. Many will repent and then be made blameless by the blood of Jesus Christ.

To the contrary, false teachers and preachers who appeal more and more to the apostasy of the corporate church, the synagogue of satan, will begin dropping like flies. If a hurricane heads their way, for just one example, they'll be killed, or their home or such will be destroyed. Because God is fed up with those who claim His name, yet, use the gospel for their own gain, or worse, take advantage of widows, and teach people lies. But false signs and lying wonders will increase just the same, including the lying phenomena of the aliens and UFOs.

So, yes, these first 3 ½ years will have great turmoil with all the disasters and increasing lawlessness, persecution, great famine, and death. But they are also a time of great evangelism and glory, wherein greater works than what Jesus had done, take place. And the troubles of these first few years are nothing compared to the indescribably thick stench of evil that's unleashed in the second half.

Now, right before the rapture happens in the middle of the seven years after the antichrist desecrates the temple in Jerusalem which, at the time of this writing, is very soon to be built, the Bible tells us there will be signs. First there will be sudden darkness and cosmic disturbance - including an asteroid hitting earth! Then, sometime shortly after this - it could be minutes, it could be days or weeks - the sky will open up like a scroll and Jesus will be seen by all who are supposed to be His! The old covenant Jews who love God but rejected Jesus will finally see Him on His throne for themselves, that He actually is the one true Messiah. And they'll be mortified because now they know judgment has come upon the earth and they're stuck in it.

It's the same for the disobedient, idolatrous Christians. Because their salvation robes are filthy with sin and such, they won't be taken in the rapture. And when the sky opens and Jesus is seen, they might get excited at first thinking here they go. But they'll be horrified moments later, or however long later, I don't know, when they see others going up, but they do not go with them! Many of them will be shocked because they are convinced they qualify to go. But they aren't because their pastors did not teach them the truth, and also because they didn't read the Bible for themselves! And they'll be so angry that some will even curse their pastors and God. Others will fortunately, finally repent. But they'll mourn in great agony in realizing how they dreadfully messed up, knowing that they'll now have to suffer living on the run from a monster that wants to torture or kill them. Which is exactly what ends up happening. Many get maliciously tortured. But they all eventually get their heads cut off.

So, once the faithful, and all those who had responded to the warnings of the watchmen with sincere repentance, are raptured in the middle of the seven years, and the Great Tribulation starts, life will be utter turmoil for those who don't take the mark of the beast. Because they know if they do, their torment will be a million times worse and will last FOREVER - which is far worse than even the agony of the Great Tribulation. They know beyond a shadow of a doubt that they must NEVER take that mark.

Now, as for the native Jews who live in Israel during the middle of the seven years, when the Great Tribulation and the invasion of Jerusalem happens, the Bible tells us ⅓ of them will be spared, that they'll flee and go into hiding in the wilderness. The antichrist does try to go after them but fails, unlike how he finds the Christians, and tortures and kills them.

During this second half of the tribulations, darkness will dominate the earth while those who follow the antichrist, though much like zombies on account of the mark installed in their bodies, are seemingly living the high life, in as much as they can, considering the ever increasing extreme weather and natural disasters all over the world. Including hot weather. It will become unbearably hot, and water will gradually dry up, because the sun will have more and more solar flares. A few years into this second half, all the people of God who had finally repented and didn't take the mark, who are called saints in the Bible in the book of Revelation, will be killed by getting their heads cut off.

After they're all safe in heaven, then God will pour out seven bowls of wrath upon the wicked people who took the mark, which will cause them all great agony. Sometime close to the end of the seven years, Jesus will come down with His army, the 144,000 who served Him as militant watchmen during the first 3 ½ years. He will come down and protect the new Jewish believers from the heat and the enemy, according to Isaiah 49:10. Sometime after Jesus arrives down here, evil spirits will gather a massive army of supernatural beings and hybrids along with humans from all around the world, to what's known as the Battle of Armageddon in the Valley of Jehoshaphat, or Kidron Valley. And Jesus will destroy them.

By this time the elements will have melted, and much of the earth will have been burned up, according to 2 Peter 3:10-12, so Jesus will make heaven and earth new. And then the new millennium will finally begin, with Jesus and His children serving Him as priests and kings over the nations of the earth. Anyone who served Jesus while on earth, or anyone who was killed or beheaded for not renouncing Jesus, will get to reign with Him in the new earth. He will give them jobs of authority over the nations. And they will be immortal, in glorified bodies, just as Jesus is, able to travel at the speed of thought.

But there will also be people who had been in hiding who didn't follow the antichrist, in addition to the Jews, who survived. And, after they've all been separated as sheep are separated from goats, as described in Matthew 25:31-46, the goats who had no heart to help, share with, or care for anyone who was in distress during the troublesome years of the tribulations, will be sent into everlasting punishment.

And all the rest of the survivors who had righteous hearts, who did help God's people in their times of need by simply providing a drink of water in some cases, will be welcomed into God's kingdom to repopulate the earth.

At this time, the earth will have been brought back to the condition it was in, in the Garden of Eden, before sin. But while the antichrist and the false prophet were thrown into the Lake of Fire after the Battle of Armageddon, Satan wasn't. He gets bound and locked up in the bottomless pit for 1000 years, and afterwards, will be released for a short while to tempt mankind one last time. The irony is, despite the Lord making the world glorious, peaceful and safe, and His granting people access to the Tree and River of life which keeps them healthy and living ongoing, some people will still succumb to evil at Satan's beckoning at the end of the thousand year reign when he's released. Satan will personally gather an evil army to attempt to take over the mighty city of Jerusalem where Jesus rules from His throne. But I don't need to tell you what happens. Okay, well, Satan fails miserably yet again. And then, according to Revelation 20:10-14, Satan is finally cast into the Lake of Fire, along with death and hell. Meaning humans can't die anymore after that. And God's mission will finally be complete - to have children who love Him and righteousness, who are also finally perfect in Him, never to sin again.

Most of the following is a reiteration of all I just shared, but I feel compelled to present these final seven years in an outline to make it a simplified reference:

I. *During the first 3 ½ years of the Seven Year Tribulation, there will be:*
    A. An accelerated, greater emphasis on **global unity** through the one world religion, global green, and SDG 2030 Agenda initiatives.
    B. A **Two-State Solution** will finally be reached, dividing GOD'S land, and the third temple of Jerusalem will finally be built. And if America played a role in this solution, many people have prophesied that the USA will experience a major earthquake through the middle that will divide the country, and drastically change everything, including the government; that the US economy will be devastated, and a new digital currency introduced.
    C. An ever-increasing breakdown of moral law, **lawlessness**, hatred and feuding.
    D. Ever-increasing extreme weather, wildfires, earthquakes and other **natural disasters.**
    E. Ever-increasing **wars and rumors of wars.**
    F. Ever-increasing pressure by the corporate Christian church for all the denominations to join the abominable, **one-world-religion** bandwagon.
    G. Ever-increasing decline in resources such as fuel and food, bringing on the **worst**

famine in all of history, which will likely peak during the 2nd, and even more so, in the 3rd year, in 2026, with several hundred billion people being killed by starvation, starving animals eating people, cannibalism, and the spread of diseases.

H. Ever-increasing death - not due to severe weather disasters or famine only, but also a **plague** of pestilence as well as a rise in **random, unexpected deaths**. I can't demonstrate this via scripture, this is coming from a knowing in my innermost being. I perceive that there are many who have received salvation through Christ but still waver in and out of faith, and would not be found "clean" at the time of the rapture. These believers would be vulnerable to deception and taking the mark of the beast, so Jesus, in His mercy, will take them before-hand. Many people of all ages will die over the first half of the tribulations simply because they do belong to Jesus and He doesn't want to lose them due to their vulnerabilities and double mindedness. Those who take the mark are eternally separated from God. So God must take them home before the middle of the seven years, before they can be tempted in this way. I believe the hundreds of millions of deaths prior to the Great Tribulation is God's sovereign hand protecting certain believers from later being won over by the beast system. It's a profound act of mercy and grace. Though all the death from the plague, famine, disasters and all else will be terrible to behold, we'll have to remember that it's for the good for many to be taken to be WITH THE LORD ahead of time. It will be painful, but we must expect this and rejoice, that concerning these vulnerable believers, they will not be lost to eternal damnation. That's what's most important!

I. Ever-increasing **supernatural events with angels and demons**. As the middle of the seven years approaches, these things will be very common, with demonic powers desperately striving to deceive believers with lying wonders, in order to deem them powerless and also to destroy them. Likewise, there will be more and more holy angels making appearances and showing up to help the people of God.

J. Ever-increasing **miraculous evangelism** with the 144,000 of Revelation 7 and 14, as well as the two Witnesses of Revelation 11, preaching of the true gospel of Jesus Christ's kingdom to the ends of the earth, in power with miracles; with many regional areas becoming supernatural glory zones, refuge centers, and light-houses of God, where millions of desperate, hurting, hungry, and frightened people flock for safety, resources, deliverance, healing, and salvation.

K. An ever-increasing **major alien deception** involving supposed extra-terrestrial and ufo's, which will be all the rave near the end of the first half, paving the way for the antichrist, who, perhaps, even claims to be the Jesus from 2000 years ago, but that he's been in outer space, or heaven, all this time waiting for the right time to come back and rule, and that all the "aliens" are his supreme beings from beyond earth.

L. And there will be **laws created against true believers**, likely during the final six to nine months, or so, of the first half of the tribulation, making it illegal to preach against the abominable, one world religion - requiring all offenders to be imprisoned or put to death.

II. *During the middle of the Seven Year Tribulation Period:*

    A. When the world has embraced the deception concerning the "aliens", and when the line between the true Christians and the apostate Christians is clearly defined, the antichrist will **desecrate the temple** that the Jews recently finished building, bringing a halt to the Jews' sacrifices and offerings.

    B. When those who are in Jerusalem see the abomination standing in the holy place, about a third will suddenly realize that the two witnesses who'd been warning about this for the past few years were telling the truth, and these **Jews will flee** to the mountains. It will likely be a Sabbath day and winter, because Jesus said to pray that this day would not occur on either of these - which to me, is a big hint. The reason they flee is because they know, based on what the two witnesses had been preaching for over 3 years, that an invasion of Jerusalem and the Great Tribulation is literally at the door.

C. Immediately, after the distress of the previous 3 ½ years and people frantically fleeing Jerusalem for their lives, there will be **signs in the sun, moon, and stars**, including an asteroid hitting earth and turning ⅓ of the water to poison and killing many.

D. After these cosmic disturbances, be it minutes, days or weeks later, the sky will open like a scroll and **Jesus will be seen in heaven** by all Jews who'd rejected Him, and all those who claim to believe in Him.

E. Simultaneous to this, Satan will have just been cast to the earth, and **he opens the bottomless pit** to release millions of supernatural evil beings; **and the four angels** locked up in the River Euphrates will be released to soon kill ⅓ of mankind, which will be about 2.5 billion people.

F. Simultaneous to all this, **persecution against the true Christians**, mainly the watchmen who are still preaching against the apostasy of the one world religion and all else, is at the highest peak in all of history, with many of them laying their lives down unto death, being imprisoned and killed.

G. And then **God will rapture** all those who are spotless, who've been atoned for by the blood of Christ on account of their sincere repentance. Jesus will descend down to the clouds with a shout and a loud trumpet; there will be an earthquake and the dead in Christ will rise from their graves, receive glorified bodies, then ascend up to meet Jesus, and then all who are alive and remain on earth who have listened to the watchmen, repented and called on the name of the Lord prior to this moment, will be changed in an instant into their glorified, perfected bodies, and will also ascend up to heaven to meet Jesus in the air. They will not have to face the Great Tribulation that's presently beginning at this time.

H. Those who have been called up to meet Jesus in the air will go before the **Bema Seat of Christ**, and receive all their rewards, as discussed in Revelation 11, and then attend the **Marriage Supper of the Lamb**, as discussed in Revelation 19.

III. *During the Great Tribulation, the second half of the seven years:*
- A. **Israel will be invaded** according to Zeccariah 14.
- B. The **antichrist will go after the Israelites** who had just fled Jerusalem, but will fail to capture them.
- C. In his fury, Revelation 12:17 tells us that the antichrist will then **go after the rest of Israel's offspring**, which are the believers who have just repented and are now on the run and hiding from him, because they know that he is out to force them to submit to him through torture, even long-term, lock them in concentration camps, and eventually, kill them for not denying Jesus and refusing to bow in allegiance to his rule. The reason Revelation 12:17 calls these believers the "rest" of Israel's offspring is because of the ones who were just raptured that He can't touch. The ones he hunts are those who believed in Jesus but were not heeding the warnings of the watchmen. They didn't believe them, that the wrath of the Lamb was about to be poured out. They were caught up in the world and themselves, idolatry and sin, and even believed the lies of the antichrist and the adulterous church - and they refused to repent. That is, until they saw Jesus on His throne when the sky parted like a scroll.

Then they knew full well what was happening, but it was too late for them.
D. Scripture also tells us in Revelation 14:8, 16:19, 17:18, and 18:10, that **the great city, Mystery Babylon, will be destroyed in one hour**. Some say this great city is Rome or the Vatican, home of the hierarchy of the Christian faith, who led the nations into false doctrines and abomination, especially with their one world religion initiative. Others say this great city is New York or the USA because, being a Christian nation, the United States has also led other nations of the world into great abominations. Meanwhile, there are others who believe these passages reflect both, since many scriptures do have dual meanings. Perhaps it does include both, because there are countless prophetic warnings of judgment coming upon America - and I see or perceive this as transpiring at the onset of the Great Tribulation - literally simultaneous to the rapture and the invasion of Israel. Likely so that America cannot come to Israel's aid. But I cannot substantiate this with scripture.
E. Simultaneous to all this, as the antichrist strives to gain control of Israel and the USA, and because of the most recent chaos of the asteroid and the millions of people disappearing in the rapture, as well as the severe famine and plague that killed

hundreds of millions of people, this is when the antichrist takes charge over the economy of the world by instituting **the mark of the beast**. Nobody will be able to participate in the economy in any fashion without it.

F. The believers, who have finally repented, spend the following three plus years **on the run and in hiding from the antichrist**. Some will be discovered, locked up in camps, and tortured throughout those few years. The weather and lack of resources will be a major hardship for those who aren't captured throughout these three plus years. Revelation 14:9-13 says those who die throughout this time are actually blessed, because it's a deliverance from the hell on the earth.

G. After a few years of this, Revelation 14:14-16 says the people of God are finally ready, or ripe, for harvest. Meaning all who were left behind and forced to choose between Jesus and the devil have done so. They have passed the test, showing they'd rather be stripped naked and made an outcast to the world, than to give up their eternal hope with Jesus. And they clearly established their resolve. This **sickling of the harvest** is when all the saints are captured and killed with their heads being cut off.

H. After the harvesting of God's people, Jesus and His army will come down to the earth.

He will land on the Mount of Olives, causing a major earthquake. He will **rescue the new Messianic Jews** and protect them from the heat and the antichrist, as the world endures extreme destruction.

I. This is when God will pour out **seven bowls of wrath** upon the wicked which include horrendous sores on everyone who took the mark of the beast. And the sun will become most unbearable at this time, simultaneous to all the drinking water in the earth drying up.

J. The devil will gather all the wicked from around the earth to come to the Valley of Jehoshaphat to what is called the **Battle of Armageddon**. Jesus will destroy them.

K. The antichrist and the false prophet will be cast into the Lake of Fire.

L. And finally, **Satan will be bound** and locked up in the bottomless pit for 1000 years; and the new millennium with the new heaven and earth, where the lion will lay down with the lamb, and with **Jesus the King ruling** from the great city, Jerusalem, will finally begin.

Chapter Four

The Final Feasts of the Lord

I know my emphasis in this letter is about the final seven years, but I want to mention the (Jewish) Feasts of the Lord, and my theory as to when the final three are fulfilled - because the timeline of these three feasts supports, or coincides with, everything else I've mentioned. This timeline discovery so amazingly complements the final seven year projection. Of course, there's always that chance that I'm mistaken. But with how this Feast timeline parallels the seven year outline, it'll be shocking if things do not play out as I suspect.

These feasts are holidays that Jews practice, but they're actually God's appointed holy days that He wanted His people to recognize every year. There are different reasons for this. One of them is because these feasts were a foreshadowing of the Lord's coming, relating to both the first coming of Christ

2000 years ago, and His second coming, which is at the door.

I promised not to complicate things so I won't thoroughly explain the nuts and bolts of God's feasts in this letter, but there are seven of them, and the first four, which occur in the spring, were fulfilled to the very day of the dates of the feasts the year that Jesus came the first time, beginning with the Feast of Passover. If you want to study this for yourself, beware and keep in mind that the majority that is taught today concerning the feasts is based on traditions that the Jews added to the original holiday.

What I'm telling you here is strictly based on the Bible, namely Leviticus 16, Leviticus 23, and Numbers 29. And the real short of everything is that the final 3 feasts, which occur in September and October of each year constitute Christ's return.

The question is, **how do these 3 different fall feasts relate to the Lord's second coming?**

These 3 holy days are called...

- The Feast of Trumpets, and it's to be celebrated the 1st day of their 7th month
- The Day of Atonement, and it's to be celebrated the 10th day of their 7th month
- The Feast of Tabernacles, and it's to be celebrated the 15th day of their 7th month

Most Christians believe that the Feast of Trumpets is indicative of the rapture of the church, and that the Day of Atonement is indicative of the judgment that God pours out on Israel and the nations before His return, and that the Feast of Tabernacles is indicative of when Jesus is with us, reigning over the earth. But I disagree with most of that.

The bottom line to how I believe these 3 feasts actually do foreshadow the Lord's return is this:

First, these 3 feasts occur in month SEVEN - and the number seven means "completion". Just as everything about the book of Revelation is in sevens. It's the book of "completion". Therefore, the fall feasts occuring in the seventh month tell me that the three of them, together, show the timestamps of the completion.

Secondly, since Jesus cannot execute 3 1/2 years of judgment, and return to earth to reign, all in a matter of 2 or 3 weeks, these days aren't indicative of days, rather, they represent years. So my theory is that, the scripture which states, "on the first day of the seventh month", this is a coded way of saying, "in the first year of the season of completion". With that being said...

- In the first year of the season of completion, God's people are to begin sounding the alarm and warn the world... that the door of atonement through Christ will soon close!

- In the tenth year of the season of completion, the door of the atonement through the shed blood of Jesus Christ closes. Those who fail to truly repent will not qualify to be taken in the rapture which transpires during this tenth year.
- In the 15th year of the season of completion, ALL of God's people will begin their eternal celebration and rejoicing with Jesus, all who had been raptured, all who had overcome the antichrist during the Great Tribulation by not taking the mark of the beast, and all of His chosen people who finally received Jesus as their Messiah. They'll finally all tabernacle together at the New Jerusalem.

Based on this, I believe the first year of the Season of Completion began in September of 2017 when the Revelation 12 sign, the constellation of Virgo, was clearly displayed in the stars. Though there have been similar alignments of these stars, September 2017 was the only time this constellation has ever appeared exactly as Revelation 12 describes.

By the way, you'll likely hear about this: In September 2023, there is, or was, by the time you're reading this, a similar presentation of this constellation of Virgo, but it is NOT the same. What they call, the "Child", in the womb of Virgo, does not retrograde for nine months. It enters Virgo's womb around August 22nd of 2023 and exits around September 16th of 2023. That's not even a full month's gestation! Meanwhile, the king of the planets, Jupiter, retrograded in Virgo's womb for nine months until September 2017. Furthermore, in the 2023 constellation, the "Child" that's in Virgo's womb is an asteroid! Yuck! Michael says it sounds like perhaps the "child" in this constellation this time is more like a short-lived shooting star, and has to do with the antichrist season being born. And if he is correct, and though it's stating the obvious, this asteroid in Virgo during the Feast of Trumpets, reveals that Virgo, meaning Israel, plays a role in the rise of the antichrist!

Meanwhile, there's another asteroid called "United Nations" that passes through Virgo's womb, literally, just before the asteroid named "Child" does. Yet, nobody seems alarmed by this. All I can think is, "Beware of the Child that follows the United Nations through Israel's womb". And that's not the half of it. Believe it or not, there's an asteroid named Francis, as in the Pope, and there's one named Ukraina, hanging out in the constellation of Virgo at this time, as well. I have a video on Youtube that shows how these two other asteroids, Saga and Alku, literally accompany the "Child" as it travels through the womb. And the meaning of these asteroids is shouting a message to the world to beware of this child. How eerie and alarming all this is!

You know, the very meaning of Yom Teruah, or what they refer to as the Feast of Trumpets, is to SHOUT. This shouting can either be for something joyous or it can be a war cry or some other cry of alarm.

Technically, this feast should be called the Feast of Shouting & Sounding the Alarm. That being said, the crazy rendition of the 2023 constellation of Virgo, occurs over the week of the "Feast of Shouting and Sounding the Alarm". Therefore, I believe this entire constellation is SHOUTING to the world that a time of great troubles are about to begin! I mean, with all these asteroid names having such negative connotations, it screams, "Danger! Warning!"

So, how can this "Child" asteroid be anything good? Especially since the story of Mary giving birth to the TRUE child, Jesus Christ and His body of believers, had already been clearly demonstrated in the 2017 constellation! The VIRGIN Mary, Virgo, cannot give birth to a second true child of God, because by the second child, she's no longer a virgin! Therefore, this "Child" is not the same child of redemption. It's an imposter. A false child! A false Messiah! –This emphatically means, then, the 2023 constellation of Virgo and her alignment with all these asteroids, and her not having the twelve prominent stars crowning her head that Revelation 12 reports, is very suspicious and disconcerting, to say the least!

And as if all that's not enough, there's this comet, Nishimura, which pierces Virgo's heart on September 19, 2023, and then disappears soon after. This comet has an affiliation with redemption because of the number it's classified by. Personally, I feel Nishimura represents the mourning that Virgo we'll experience when the day of the rapture does come, after the sky opens as a scroll, and she sees the Lamb of God at the right hand of the Father, in Heaven, and it hits her how wrong she had been in her rejection of the Christ. This, in my opinion, is the only way something affiliated with redemption, such as the comet Nishimura, could ever be a thing that would pierce Virgo's heart - aside from when Simeon told Mary that a sword would pierce her soul back when Jesus was a baby, in Luke 2:35.

But because of Nishimura, as well as the asteroid named "Child" which passes through Virgo's womb over the course of a few weeks, numerous people are declaring that the September 2023 sign in the stars suggests a 2023 to 2024 rapture. But it doesn't. I assure you. Not only does this not line up with the scripture's very clear depiction of the timing of the rapture, which is not for about another 3 ½ or more years from September 2023, but these eerie asteroids which are all up in Virgo's business, are flat out disturbing to me. They feel that because this asteroid, called "Child", is the exact term used in Revelation 12, as opposed to calling it "Jupiter", that this means this 2023 rendition and its child represents the church being born and raptured. But this is wrong!

My thoughts are that God set this up, in order to warn of the rise of a false child that's trailing behind the United Nations - but makes his youthful, subtle entrance around September 19, 2023. I believe God wants us to pay attention to the fact that the asteroid Child isn't in the womb for 9 months like a real human - the way Jupiter was. How can we negate that? True, it doesn't say "Jupiter" in Revelation 12, but "Child. But it's astronomical that the KING planet hangs around in Virgo's womb for 9 months! That's amazing! So, we should not shrug the rendition of 2017 off just because the rapture didn't occur then. But instead, embrace the real point of that sign.

And, you know what else? Based on the craziness of the false Child asteroid actually being in Virgo's womb at all, my suspicion is that this "Child" just might claim that he's the one that was born of the virgin Mary 2000 years ago. That he is back now. And he might also say the aliens are the ones who impregnated the virgin Mary with him. Time will tell!

Take a look at these constellations of Virgo from the Stellarium website on the following page. Two of the images are from 2017's rendition, and the third is from 2023. Have Revelation 12:1-5 open as you review these illustrations.

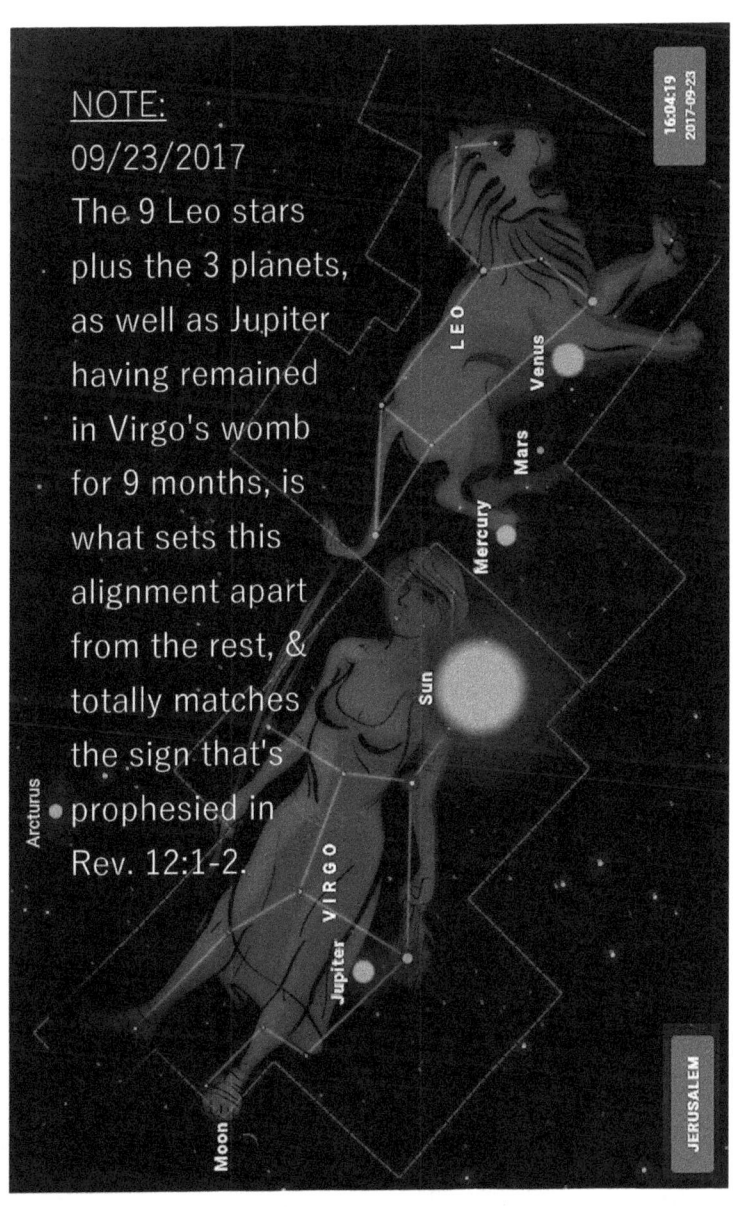

NOTE:
09/23/2017
The 9 Leo stars plus the 3 planets, as well as Jupiter having remained in Virgo's womb for 9 months, is what sets this alignment apart from the rest, & totally matches the sign that's prophesied in Rev. 12:1-2.

stellarium-web.org/

Above is another image of the 2017 alignment, this time showing the fiery dragon waiting to devour the king planet (Jupiter) which had been in Virgo's womb since November 2016. Again, exactly as Revelation 12 describes. Meanwhile, below you see in the 2023 alignment, the sun is in her hair, not clothing her body. The moon isn't snug with her feet. And there are only 10 prominent stars, Leo's + Mercury, above her head unless you count the additional 3 less significant stars, which makes 13 total, not 12. This is NOT the alignment from Revelation 12. It's a COUNTERFEIT that warns of the rise of a FALSE MESSIAH! — Not the rapture. Beware of the Child that follows the United Nations.

Unfortunately I wasn't able to squeeze all the other asteroids that are hanging out with Virgo, into this small illustration. Just know that the main differences, outside of the numerous asteroids, is that there are not 12 prominent stars above her head in 2023's version; and the "Child" she gives birth to isn't human, because it didn't spend nine months in her womb, like Jupiter had done in 2017!

But back to the point, again, many voices on social media are saying 2023's version, with the eerie asteroid passing through Virgo's womb called "Child", also, if not more so, reflects the Revelation 12 sign, and, therefore, suggests that this is a sign that the rapture is about to occur. So as I write this, many born again believers literally expect Jesus to come get them between now and the end of 2024. The bottom line, however, is there's no way a 3 week asteroid fetus represents the church being raptured. Not at all. Therefore, what these folks will hopefully realize by the end of 2024, is that this 2023 sign in the constellation of Virgo, is actually about the rise of the antichrist. And they'll hopefully also realize the need to prepare to die for Jesus for preaching the truth when the law, a couple years later, will forbid it. Yes, this will be the case maybe late 2026 but definitely by early 2027.

Now back to my theory about the timeline of the final three feasts of God. Since the constellation of Virgo totally reflected the unique description that's outlined in Revelation 12 in September of 2017, I believe it's the sign that marks something huge, such as the onset of the fulfillment of these final feasts. Think about it. The Bible is loaded with prophecy. But Revelation 12 literally paints a picture of this one-time occurrence in the heavens for a reason, because it points to an extremely significant moment in the timeline of Christ's return. We're talking about a passage in the Bible that was written 2000 years ago. For God to highlight this very specific constellation, then this means that the moment it appears, we should recognize that it's to be a notable, key date in the end-times timeline. And, I repeat, the 2017 constellation unmistakably reflects Revelation 12, not 2023's. Yes, 2023's crazy rendition has become all the rave, and for good reason. It is "a" sign, too. But it isn't "the" sign that's recorded in the holy Bible.

But why? Why did God allow two very astronomical Virgo constellation signs to occur six years apart, but only mention one of them in the Bible?

The reason is, again, because the 2017 rendition marks one of the most significant moments in history, which is the very commencement of the fulfillments of the final three holy feasts of God. Thus, making it the first year of the "season of completion". Meaning, day one of the seventh month, which is the Feast of Trumpets, or Alarms, began when the REAL Revelation 12 sign occurred in September of 2017!

I cannot prove this theory, but we can consider what such a timetable would look like.

If the first year begins September 2017, then the tenth year, which is the Day of Atonement, would begin by September 2026, and last through to September 2027. And then the fifteenth year would begin on the Feast of Tabernacles in 2031, when, after making the heaven and earth new, Jesus brings down the New Jerusalem. This lines up with my summary of how the final seven years will go… perfectly.

Remember, I outlined that once the covenant with many is established, be it the SDG, or the Two State Solution, this is when the final seven years begin. And, I outlined that the rapture happens very soon after the abomination of desolation in the middle of the seven years. So, when I place these final seven years on a timeline next to the feast date years from 2017 through 2031, they match my seven year projection perfectly. The illustration on page 61 shows the various events that have occurred and have yet to occur. Check out how the feast "years" timeline coincides with the final seven years' events:

And note that from September 2030 through September 2031, that this is AFTER Jacob's Trouble has ended. It's important to realize that the final seven years strictly concern God addressing Israel – both DNA Jews, and the disobedient church that was grafted into the vine. Daniel's 70th week isn't about God's judgment upon Satan's kingdom in the earth. It's strictly upon His people. And it's after He relents disciplining His people, after the rest of the wheat is sickled, see Revelation 14 and 15, and He comes down to personally deliver the Jews, see Zechariah 14:4 and Isaiah 49:8-26, that He pours out the bowls of judgment and wrath upon Satan's kingdom in the earth. And it's during the year after Jacob's Trouble ceases that the battle of Armageddon comes to pass. In other words, there's a final seven years for the people of God. Then Jesus takes the time to wrap things up with the antichrist and the rest of the evil in the world. Then He separates the sheep from the goats. And then He makes the heavens and earth new because it's been terribly burned up by this point. And then, He brings down the New Jerusalem - which is the Feast of Tabernacles, October 1, 2031.

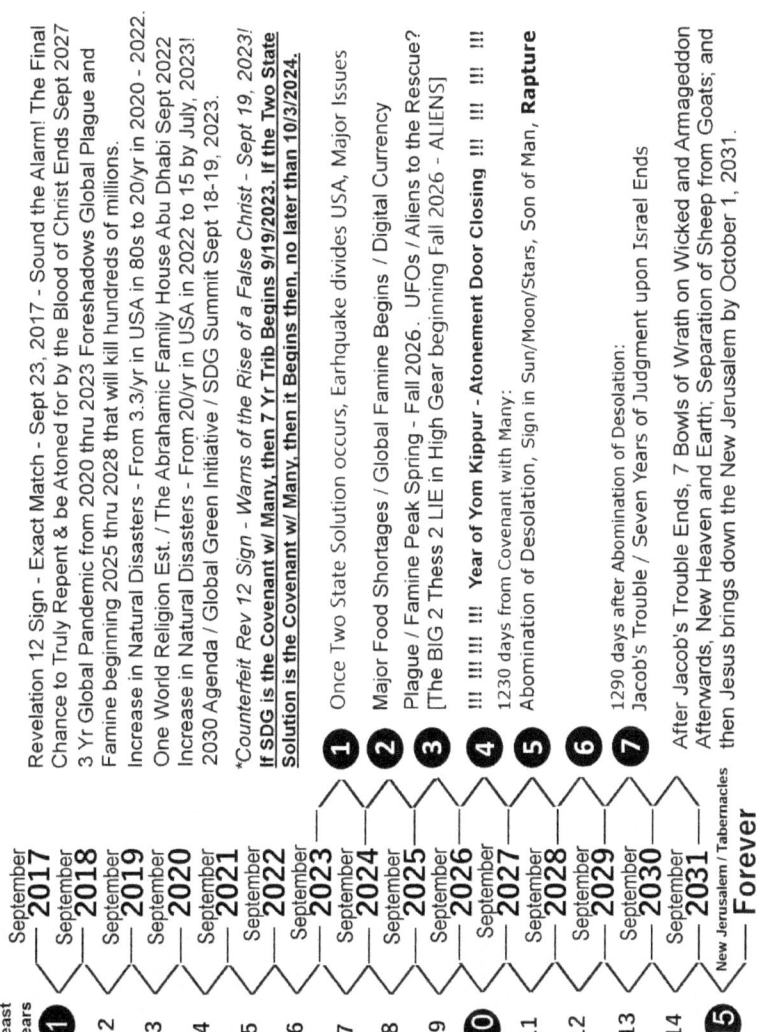

PROJECTION OF FINAL SEVEN YEARS
Fulfillment of Final Three Fall Feasts of The Lord Yr 1 thru Yr 15

Feast Years

1. September 2017 — Revelation 12 Sign - Exact Match - Sept 23, 2017 - Sound the Alarm! The Final Chance to Truly Repent & be Atoned for by the Blood of Christ Ends Sept 2027
2. September 2018 — 3 Yr Global Pandemic from 2020 thru 2023 Foreshadows Global Plague and Famine beginning 2025 thru 2028 that will kill hundreds of millions.
3. September 2019 — Increase in Natural Disasters - From 3.3/yr in USA in 80s to 20/yr in 2020 - 2022.
4. September 2020 — One World Religion Est. / The Abrahamic Family House Abu Dhabi Sept 2022
5. September 2021 — Increase in Natural Disasters - From 20/yr in USA in 2022 to 15 by July, 2023!
6. September 2022 — 2030 Agenda / Global Green Initiative / SDG Summit Sept 18-19, 2023.
7. September 2023 — *Counterfeit Rev 12 Sign - Warns of the Rise of a False Christ - Sept 19, 2023! If SDG is the Covenant w/ Many, then 7 Yr Trib Begins 9/19/2023. If the Two State Solution is the Covenant w/ Many, then it Begins then, no later than 10/3/2024.*

❶ September 2024 — Once Two State Solution occurs, Earthquake divides USA, Major Issues
❷ September 2025 — Major Food Shortages / Global Famine Begins / Digital Currency
❸ September 2026 — Plague / Famine Peak Spring - Fall 2026. UFOs / Aliens to the Rescue? [The BIG 2 Thess 2 LIE in High Gear beginning Fall 2026 - ALIENS]
❹ September 2027 — !!! !!! !!! !!! **Year of Yom Kippur - Atonement Door Closing** !!! !!! !!! !!!
❺ September 2028 — 1230 days from Covenant with Many: Abomination of Desolation, Sign in Sun/Moon/Stars, Son of Man, **Rapture**
❻ September 2029
❼ September 2030 — 1290 days after Abomination of Desolation: Jacob's Trouble / Seven Years of Judgment upon Israel Ends

⓯ September 2031 — After Jacob's Trouble Ends, 7 Bowls of Wrath on Wicked and Armageddon Afterwards, New Heaven and Earth; Separation of Sheep from Goats; and then Jesus brings down the New Jerusalem by October 1, 2031.

New Jerusalem / Tabernacles — Forever

Though I honestly tried to not go too deep into this subject, it's imperative that you understand what's going on. Especially concerning the Day of Atonement. Because THAT is the bottom line of the ENTIRE POINT to the troubles of the last days. To SAVE as many souls as possible!

As I said, most people believe the Day of Atonement represents God's judgment. But that's not the case. Judgment is the, "result", of not being atoned for on the Day of Atonement. Understand, Yom Kippur, or the Day of Atonement, was the highest holy day of the year, and the people had to afflict their own souls, by fasting and praying, while the high priest would go into the most holy place, to make atonement for them, in order to have the entire sin of the nation forgiven and washed away. For the atonement to occur, the people had to be in a genuine place of soulful remorse over their sin, which is what is meant by God telling them to afflict their souls. I'm not sure how they brought themselves into soulful anguish, but that's what God told them to do. This may be why the Jews have this tradition where they spend the previous 9 days fasting and repenting, calling the entire period, the "10 Days of Awe". They'd spend the entire ten days righting their wrongs, fasting, praying a great deal, and repenting.

The thing is, though, ever since Jesus shed His blood for all sin, He has been the only means of atonement. So, we're supposed to realize that the significance that the Day of Atonement has in relation to Christ's second coming, is that it's the day, or year, when great affliction occurs, whereby hopefully all people will have sincerely, and soulfully, repented, corrected their ways, of their own volition, in submission to Christ, to be atoned for by the blood of the Lamb -- BEFORE the Day of Judgment begins. Those who have not afflicted their souls by this time, who haven't been made clean by the atoning blood of Christ, will be left behind to endure the horrors of the Great Tribulation.

So please see... the Day of Atonement is not the judgment. It's meant to be the day, or year, when everyone has their last chance to be atoned for, just as that day was dedicated to accomplishing for the Jews in ancient times. Because for those who did not afflict their souls and repent, the Bible says they were cut off. In other words, if the devastations of the next few years don't sober people up, humble them, and beckon them to forget the lusts of their flesh, abominable lifestyles and spiritual adultery, then they'll be left to face the Great Tribulation wherein they'll not only be stripped naked of ALL their idols, but access to the basic essentials of life, to boot!

All that to say, I believe we are currently living in the 10 "Years" of Awe. And now is the time we all must desperately repent and get right with God. We need to get into complete unity with Him and His Spirit, because that's the only way all the upcoming terrors will not be able to touch us. And we'll be safe in the 10th year while, sadly, of the people who have NOT afflicted themselves by that time, hundreds of millions of them will suffer horrifically, die, or worse, will have to watch their loved ones suffer and die.

Here is something to seriously think about:

Imagine two people, be it best friends, relatives, or a married couple, who deeply love each other, sitting together at a park enjoying one another. They packed an amazing picnic lunch and they are extremely hungry because they hiked to the park. They want to eat but cannot because a passerby stopped to talk to them for a while. Finally, the passerby leaves and they excitedly lay out the blanket, pour their drinks, and are about to take their first bites of food. Both of their mouths are watering because of how famished they feel, and because they packed their favorites. And just when they're about to take their first bites, a wild animal appears out of nowhere! It grabs one of them and mauls them to death in a matter of minutes, carrying parts of their body off into the woods. I apologize for being so gruesome, but it's necessary to make the point. Because this is precisely the level of horror the world will soon face! Now, the one that wasn't attacked who dreadfully failed to save the other, is sitting there, alone, in shock and mortified. The food that they were about to devour still sits before the survivor. My question is... Does he or she still want it? Is it possible for them to eat it after what's just happened? NO! Their soul is in utter anguish!

With what just transpired, they likely don't even have the will to live! Suddenly their desire to enjoy anything, be it a meal, a movie, a vacation, their riches, their fancy car, their favorite sports and activities, their new dream job... is all lost to them. None of it matters!

Though this is the extreme, it is what it means for one's soul to be in affliction. And it's on this Day of Atonement, being the holiest day of the year, when the nation of God is supposed to corporately afflict their souls themselves, on behalf of their disdain and anguish over the horrors of sin, which plague them, and the earth. Of course, such anguish is not as excruciating as watching a loved one be mauled to death. But it's supposed to be along the same lines. Sin is to be seen as deplorable to us as watching a loved one be mauled. We are to lament over sin, deeply.

This is what qualifies one to be atoned for by the blood of Christ. This is the purpose for the Year of Atonement. It's to give everyone their final chance to demonstrate, at heart level, that they are NOT okay with being a sinner. Believers who've soiled their salvation garments will have them made white and clean again, and they will not be in danger of the great afflictions occuring around the globe. Nor, as I said, will they be in danger of having to endure the Great Tribulation that's soon to begin by this time.

To the contrary, those who are not in anguish over the depravity of the world and their own sin, will lose their last chance to be forgiven for their sins or to have their robes made white. Once this "Year" of Atonement has passed, it will be too late to be atoned for, or redeemed by the Lamb of God. From then on, all who finally come to their senses who realize their sin against a holy God, and repent of it, because they want to spend eternity with Him, will have to suffer through the Great Tribulation, denying the mark of the beast in the name of Jesus Christ.

This is a dragged out test because some will still be torn between their love for the things of this world versus their love for righteousness and God. They know if they take the mark of the beast, they'll be instantly and permanently separated from God forever. It seems it should be easy to not take it. But, how badly do they miss their ability to go shopping, or climb the corporate ladder of success? How desperate are they to solve their inability to buy whatever they want, to own a house or a car, or take a vacation? Their problems would be solved instantly with their simply agreeing to take the mark. Worse yet, how strong will they be when the enforcers stand over their children threatening to remove their heads if they don't take the mark?

This is why we must get right with God and begin afflicting our own souls, or crucifying our flesh, NOW, by laying down our idols, lusts, and all other sin, and become fully submitted to holiness by the power of Christ and the atonement He provides by His shed blood! So that we won't have to be here to face such excruciating circumstances. He doesn't want that for us! For those left behind, it will not be easy to refuse the mark of the beast! But, if they truly want to be with God forever, they will HAVE TO REJECT IT. This is the only way to make it to heaven from there on out.

But all your sins can be washed away right now, before all these terrors ensue. So that you'll be protected over these next few years while the disasters increase. And to be safe when the great famine and plague comes. Those who are not covered by the Shadow of the Almighty will be terribly affected one way or another over these next few years. But what's more terrible is that once the "Year" of Atonement has come and gone, and that door is closed, it's too late.

So I beg of you to heed what I'm telling you. The sooner you do, the safer you'll be.

Chapter Five

The Rise of the Beast

Now, it's easy to see how the antichrist can begin rising to power. But I want to explain in more detail how I believe this is happening, though behind the scenes, it's right in front of us. It's important to know this because, as you watch all this unfold, you will be far more alert to the danger of the times. And hopefully able to enlighten others. So here's how all this is working, and currently underway.

You may not be aware unless you stay on top of world news and statistics, but there are more natural disasters occurring all over the planet than ever; even more than we realize. The National Centers for Environmental Information has an article which can be found at www.ncei.noaa.gov/access/billions/ which states, *"The U.S. has sustained 363 weather and climate disasters since 1980 where overall damages reached or exceeded one billion dollars."* Of these 363 US disasters, not including other nations, there were 33, or 3.3 disasters per year, in the 1980s; there were 57, or 5.7 per year, in the 1990s; there were 67, or 6.7 per year, in the 2000s; there were 131, nearly double!, or 13.1 per year, in the 2010s; and from 2020 through 2022, there were 20 severe, billion dollar disasters, each year! So under 4 per year in the 80s, but 20 per year in 2020! Again, this being in the United States alone. And then, in another article which may be found at w t h r dot com, entitled, <u>"Record Number of Billion-Dollar Disasters for US in 2023 So Far"</u>, they report that from January to July 2023 there have already been 15 major disasters in the US alone. It states, *"That's the highest number of billion-dollar disasters ever recorded for the first seven months of a year since NOAA began tracking events in 1980."*.

The reason I start with this is because climate change is a prominent platform through which the antichrist plans to rise to power. We've been listening to the world blame climate change and global warming for decades for the insane rise in natural disasters. There's a big reason for this! The antichrist system, as in the leaders who have been under the spirit of antichrist's control, are using "climate change" and "global warming" to lay the groundwork for a one world, global government.

The thing is, the Bible tells us the final seven years begin when the antichrist confirms a covenant with many. But in order for that covenant to be made, there needs to be pre-existing, unified cooperation among the various nations. Climate change and global warming is the supposed root or reason for all our problems, and is what antichrist uses to bring these nations together. It's all a ploy.

Unbeknownst to the majority of the world, a 15 year global agreement was made in 2015 by the UN, concerning a global initiative called the Sustainable Development Goals, or, SDG. Their supposed plan is that by 2030, ironically, all their goals for the supposed "well-being of the world" will have been met. The SDG appears to be a powerful plan that will make the world a better place, promising peace and safety. Incase you are interested, it includes the following 17 goals:

1. no poverty
2. zero hunger
3. good health and well-being
4. quality education
5. gender equality
6. clean water and sanitation
7. affordable and clean energy
8. decent work and economic growth
9. industry, innovation and infrastructure
10. reduced inequalities
11. sustainable cities and communities
12. responsible consumption and production
13. climate action
14. life below water (well-being)
15. life on land (well-being)
16. peace, justice, and strong institutions
17. and partnerships for the goals

While it's questionable what on earth gender equality has to do with preserving and improving the world, it seems all the rest are a noble cause. The problem is... This initiative, which many countries are already in a legal binding agreement with, is an indirect step towards a one world government - and its ruler. Because even though no kings or rulers say they want someone else ruling them, they're being subtly primed for it. This SDG is merely the framework. So when the day comes that catastrophic events strike the earth, threatening their so-called Sustainable Development Goals initiative, they're going to have to give their power over to a one world ruler! Which is precisely the plan. The antichrist is counting on the major disasters and economic devastations that the Bible prophesied, in order to finally have a reason, with many nations of the world primed, for him to come to the rescue!

First of all, the elite behind the SDG are personally behind the breakdown of world economic systems, causing inflation and a reduction in resources, namely food and fuel; and soon, much needed medications, and more. But secondly, like I said, the spirit behind this agenda, which is laying out the red carpet for the rise of a one world leader, knows that the Holy Bible warns of increasing natural disasters at the time of the end, which you can see in Matthew 24:6-8, and Mark 13:7-8. So he, the devil and the people implementing his plans, will use the devastations of the natural disasters, and all the other socio-economic distresses of earth, as the antichrist's launch pad to power. Then, when the time is right and the earth is in dire straits, this little guy from the side-lines will have all the answers, and will become highly esteemed. He will likely be a middle-eastern Muslim based on my research, and will shine like an amazing star in dark times. He will have an astonishing, and even mesmerizing, message of peace and solutions to all the troubles impacting the world. And he will be marveled over according to Revelation 13:3, and Revelation 17:8.

In Matthew 24, Jesus said there will be profound deception at the time of the rise of antichrist, so much so, that even God's true followers will believe it. I'll explain more about this later, but for now, I want you to understand the point that this eloquent, charming global leader will convince nearly everyone that he is one of the most wonderful men to walk the face of the earth. In fact, he will claim to be god, the Messiah, himself! And the world will believe it! He will be astonishing and seemingly wonderful! But he is 100% of the devil and must not be believed. All who follow him and take his mark to buy, sell, and trade, will experience incomprehensible torment with agonizing sores all over their bodies (see Revelation 16:1-2). And that's just the beginning. They will then suffer with unbearable heat as the sun goes berserk. On top of that, all the water sources will dry up on earth. The worst of all is they will ultimately be thrown into the Lake of Fire. And in the eternal state, people feel things a thousand times more than on earth. Take your worst fears and worst pain on earth that you ever had, and multiply it to infinity. This is the torment these people will endure.

How can a good God allow or do this? Putting it simply, this is the fate for all those who, after seven years of chastisement and God practically begging them to choose holiness and repent, they don't! They hate God. But last I checked, it's HIS WORLD. Who are we to question Him? Anyone that can hate the wonder, beauty and goodness of a Holy God, who could defy a God that let evil people partake of His wondrous creation, food, water, and resources, and who could despise a God who allowed His creation to spit on Him, whip Him to shreds, and nail Him to a tree just so He could reconcile them to righteousness and the Father... deserves to be destroyed.

Back to the point... Understand that there are other moving parts to this well-oiled, beast-system-machine, which will pave the way for the rise of the antichrist. Such as the new found one world religion which Pope Francis brought to the table. This one World Religion headquarters, called The Abrahamic Family House, consists of a Muslim mosque, a Christian church, and a Jewish Synagogue. These three faiths are all from the descendents of Abraham: Ishmael and Isaac. It was built on an island in the middle eastern city of Abu

Dhabi, and Pope Francis, the "overseer" of the Christian faith, though more specifically, over Roman Catholicism, and Sunni Muslim leader, Sheikh Ahmen al-Tayeb, both signed the Document of Human Fraternity for World Peace. This document is a **global peace agreement**! And this was set into place in 2022! I'm pretty sure you understand that this is an abomination to the very core of Christianity because Jesus Christ and His shed blood is the only WAY to eternal paradise, while the other two faiths under Abraham are not. Therefore, unity with these faiths might seem like a swell thing to do in the name of peace. But it isn't. This one world religious system is anti-truth; antichristian. It's the root of the great apostasy spoken of in 2 Thessalonians 2:3. But more than all that, it is a major building block in the one world government plot which is gaining greater momentum with every second that passes. -Governments know that uniting religions is key in acquiring global control. So that's why the Pope ushered in this false religious system, whether he realizes it, or not.

Now back to the SDG, this global initiative towards world peace and well-being was first established and signed by many nations in 2015. But here's the situation... Because of the drastic rise in the catastrophic disasters in the world these past few years, and because this year marks the middle of this 15 year initiative, leaving only seven years until 2030, until the goals are supposed to be achieved, they are holding an SDG Summit on September 18-19, 2023. The following is a quote from the United Nations website:

"It, the summit, will mark the beginning of a new phase of **accelerated progress** towards the Sustainable Development Goals with **high-level political guidance** on transformative and **accelerated actions** leading up to 2030. Convened by the President of the General Assembly, the Summit will mark the half-way point to the deadline set for achieving the 2030 Agenda and the Sustainable Development Goals. It will be the centerpiece of the High-level Week of the General Assembly. **It will respond to the impact of multiple and interlocking crises facing the world** and is expected to reignite a sense of hope, optimism, and enthusiasm for the 2030 Agenda."

Antonio Gutteres, the United Nations Secretary-General, stated, "The SDG Summit in September must be a moment of unity to provide a renewed impetus and accelerated actions for reaching the SDGs.".

Meanwhile, the Bible says in Daniel 9:27 that he, the antichrist system, will CONFIRM a seven year covenant with many. The question is: is the strengthening and acceleration of the SDG covenant the same covenant of Daniel 9:27?

Again, the SDG covenant was first established in 2015 but now, as of September 18-19 of 2023, at the SDG Summit in New York, this covenant is being accelerated and will need to be confirmed, which very well could be Daniel's covenant. And it's timing couldn't be more peculiar, as the summit is scheduled to begin the very day AFTER the Jewish Feast of Trumpets - which is God's required sacred time of sounding the ALARM OF WARNING TO REPENT, AND TO PREPARE FOR THE UPCOMING DAY OF ATONEMENT! It's everyone's last chance!

But as of the time of this writing, we do not know for sure what the covenant with many is. It could also pertain to the upcoming two-state solution that everyone is pushing for. Israel might need to agree to dividing God's land in order to be able to build their third temple in peace.

Regardless of what this literal covenant with many is, and when it will actually be confirmed, we can see that with the one world religion headquarters already having been established in 2022, the SDG 2030 Agenda acceleration transpiring in September 2023, which totally builds upon the antichrist's one world government platform, the up and coming two-state solution finally being reached, and not to mention the capacity for a one world currency to finally be put into place, the rise of the antichrist is most certainly underway.

Chapter Six
Many Won't Believe It's the End

I cannot prove this, it's just what I perceive in my knowing, or gut, as some might say, but I suspect that many people who call themselves Christians, won't believe that the tribulation has begun, once it actually has. The main reason I think this is because 2 Thessalonians 2 tells us that there is going to be a great falling away from the Christian faith. So it stands to reason, if they're able to be deceived and fall away from the truth of the Bible, then they likely won't understand that Jesus is about to come back and clean everything up.

But more than this, there are many conflicting and even opposing teachings about Bible prophecy and the end times. Christians have been divided for decades over how they think the scriptures report things will unfold. The most common belief is that before the seven years of tribulation even begin, there will be a rapture, and that all Christians will be taken out of the earth instantly. Now, it's true, there absolutely will be a rapture as I stated already. Christians will be removed from the earth. But NOT until the MIDDLE of the seven years, and it won't be all Christians, rather, just the ones who don't have filth on their salvation robes. However, the teachers who are preaching that Jesus will come get all Christians before the seven years even begins, call it a pre-tribulation rapture. It's a false doctrine. I prove this in my other book, as well as on my Youtube channel.

Now, because they are convinced they will be raptured before the seven year tribulation starts, I suspect that many of these Christians will say, *"No, this can't be the seven year tribulation period because we're still here! We would be gone if the tribulations actually started!"* -Wrong.

The reason I'm telling you this is because if I am correct, you will likely run into Christians who deny that the tribulation has begun. This might cause you to doubt the truth - that it most certainly has. If you do hear anyone stating this, you can bet they are pre-tribulation rapture believers. If that is the case, please guide them to my free youtube videos at the Last Days Witness Youtube channel, which totally disproves the pre-tribulation rapture theory. They are in danger. They don't think they are, though. They say, "Hey, we're prepared so if Jesus comes to get us, we will be taken in the rapture. We have nothing to worry about!" But I wonder, if they're wrong about the rapture, what else could they be wrong about? And how does Jesus feel about it? The Bible says that Jesus will tell many people who sincerely believe they are Christians and saved, and even think they're spotless, "Depart from Me! I never knew you!". The ones He says this to will be left behind to endure the Great Tribulation.

As for you, if you see that Christians don't seem alarmed about the end being upon us, despite all the proof I've laid out, which thoroughly demonstrates the hour we are in, that great judgment literally is at the door, then beware of these people!

And like I said above, I strongly suspect that the reason the corporate church, as a whole, will reject the notion that the tribulation has begun, is because 2 Thessalonians 2 tells us there will be a great apostasy, or falling away, from the true faith and teachings of Christ, involving a major lie from the son of perdition, or antichrist. Again, if Christians can believe the lie of the devil and the big deception which Jesus warned about in Matthew 24, which will have to do with aliens and possibly them being our creators, or whatever story they postulate, then this means they don't know the very Bible which warned them of all this! And they'll actually believe that the antichrist is the Messiah!

Of course, because the pre-tribulation rapture teachers are familiar with a lot of the Bible, this means they do know about the warning to not believe this lie. They know that Jesus said the only way He will come back to earth is in the clouds as lightning is seen as far as the east is from the west (see Matthew 24:26-27). Meaning, the pre-tribulation rapture teachers know that when the antichrist claims to be the Messiah!", it cannot possibly be the real Jesus, because Jesus descends down in the clouds.

Yet, though the pre-tribulation rapture teachers know of this warning, are they teaching it? Are they warning their followers and congregations? No! Why not? The reason they're not warning people is because they think, and tell everyone, they'll ALL BE GONE by the time of this great deception! All they're preaching is, *"Glory to God, we get to escape the tribulation! Praise the Lord! Be ready because Jesus is coming any minute!"*

Instead of sobering up the body of Christ and warning them of the severe persecution during the first 3 ½ years, and the call for the church to preach the truth in power to the rest of the world, even unto death, they're all excited that Jesus is about to snatch them up before all this. They have no concept that they're supposed to be here to serve the Lord in the earth's greatest hours of need, to help bring in a great harvest, and pull as many people as possible out of the thralls of the up and coming terrors.

Therefore, all these believers are aware of, is that judgment is coming, but they're safe because they're out of here before it starts. The end. No worries. Don't bother learning about the deception. So I suspect, then, as the seven years of tribulation are underway, unless their teachers publicly renounce the lie of a pre-tribulation rapture and begin warning of the deception right away, these followers who don't read the Bible for themselves are primed to believe this charming, amazing false Christ who supposedly comes to save the world from all the turmoil.

So all that to say, don't expect the majority of the church to be acting like the judgment has begun. But as you see all the things unfold that I wrote about, know beyond a shadow of a doubt that it has. And make sure you are right with God! Because those who are right with God, who walk in obedience and repentance, are abiding in the shadow of the Almighty, according to Psalm 91. This means even though a thousand are killed at their side, and ten thousand die at their right hand, no harm will come upon them. They will have protection from the disasters and the enemy - until their assignment is complete. Then, and only then, the antichrist will be able to kill them, which is actually their one way ticket to Paradise, and nothing to be afraid of whatsoever. Meanwhile, those who belong to God who are in disobedience, will suffer painful consequences for the sake of bringing them into order. The sooner they repent, the better off they'll be. And I must reiterate that any suffering at the hand of the devil that anyone faces, because they won't submit to him or deny Jesus, will only bring these people of God great, great reward.

But as for the pre-tribulation rapture believers, as of the time of this writing over the summer of 2023, they are all over social media announcing, *"Look out! Be ready, church family! It looks like the seven year tribulation is about to begin at any moment, so we know He's going to come get us any second!"* They are truly excited because they think they're about to make their exit. But they'll still be here after it begins. I can only pray they recognize the truth and get on board with Jesus, and the call of believers to preach the gospel of the kingdom to the ends of the earth in power and glory, serving as hospitals and lighthouses to the lost and hurting, bringing the masses into salvation... before the rapture does occur... in the *middle* of the tribulation period.

Chapter Seven

The Tribulations are Necessary

As I said earlier, there are many different interpretations of what the last days look like. Some say "Daniel's 70th week", which is the seven year tribulation I've been talking about as described in Daniel 9, isn't correct teaching. That there are not seven years of "judgment". But understand - there absolutely is a final week, or seven years, that will transpire, right before Jesus comes. I have studied a great deal and see how all the prophecies, together, fit into a seven year timeframe. And the entire theme and heart of the Bible requires that this seven years of turmoil take place. Otherwise the Word of God, to date, has all been pointless.

In order to understand the necessity behind these final years of global distress, we must first realize the whole point of God's plan from the beginning.

As we well know, God created mankind in His image, people who would be His family and be with Him forever. But since He didn't want robots who operated according to holiness automatically by some program, but rather, a people who loved Him, and holiness, of their own volition, He knew He had to give man free will and allow them to come to this resolve for themselves. He wouldn't force anyone to love what is right and pure, including Him. But in doing this, He knew it also meant man, even the ones that love God, could still fail and mess up, and that this would separate them from Him. Because everything He creates can only dwell in His majestic presence, if it's of the same substance. Everything that's not pure is outside of holiness, and incompatible with Him and His eternal realm. And it's only able to exist temporarily, during this 6000 years which have been granted for mankind to choose the light - or darkness. Afterwards, darkness will become obsolete; non-existent. It will all be destroyed.

So God knew full well from the start that He'd have to do something to reconcile humanity back to perfect righteousness and glory, wherein we could exist eternally with Him. And He also knew from the beginning that He would have to be the one to cleanse us with His holy blood, from the unholy condition which free will perpetuates. This meant that in order for God to complete His plan, that before He could return to earth to reign and rule, and dwell with His beloved, holy family, He'd need to crack down on humanity, warning us when time was up, chastising and disciplining us, and doing everything possible to drive us to repentance, so that the blood He shed could cleanse us all… BEFORE He comes and destroys all those who sadly, and strangely, hate Him and righteousness; those who truly are of the devil.

So there are no two ways about it. The final seven years of "judgment", which serves to distinguish those who belong to God from the lovers of darkness, MUST transpire! I hesitate to even call it judgment because the actual judgment will take place at the great White Throne down the road, when everyone will stand before Him and He will decide, then, based on all the records in the books, including the book of Life, who will remain with Him, and who will go into the eternal burning Lake of Fire. Which, for the lovers of darkness, should be to their pleasure, since they love such horrific things. They'll finally be in their ideal environment.

Unlike the White Throne Judgment when any chance for all of humanity to be reconciled with God is taken away permanently, the troubles of the final seven years are chastisement, like getting punished by parents. The parents don't destroy the children, casting them out of the family forever. Discipline is not that. And neither are the final seven years. It's the time that, for those who won't see the many signs that He's coming, who won't listen to the watchmen such as myself, they must be taken to the woodshed, so that they'll hopefully finally repent and then be able to be with God in paradise forever. And the first 3 ½ years, though severe, aren't as horrific and demonic as the second half. This is because there are some people who will repent with minor discipline. But there are others who need a stronger hand of punishment before they will repent. And sadly, there are people who will need the horrific severity of the Great Tribulation before they'll finally repent.

If everyone would repent right now, these seven years of tribulation would not be necessary. And if God didn't care about us, and was okay with just a few people being fully reconciled to Him, then the seven years of tribulation would, likewise, not be necessary. But He loves us so much. He must go to whatever extremes necessary to beckon mankind to be cleansed by the blood of Jesus Christ. And the troubles will become progressively worse - because of the ones who are more stubborn. God loves and wants them desperately. Therefore, the seven final years are God taking drastic measures to wash people clean, so that as many people as possible can be with Him forever.

Now, I want you to understand that the Great Tribulation, or Jacob's Trouble, that I've been talking about, accounts for the majority of what the Bible calls, "the great and terrible Day of the Lord". I won't lay the scriptures out here to prove how this is so, but, while some scholars teach that this "Day of the Lord" occurs at the very end of the seven years only, after Jacob's Trouble, and while other scholars strangely, despite zero Biblical substantiation, teach that it encompasses the entire seven years, I can scripturally prove that the "Day of the Lord" begins with Jacob's Trouble, as in the Great Tribulation, and that it starts in the middle of the seven years, and goes through to the end. And it's this, "Day of the Lord", which is God's chastisement upon, first, His people, Israel, and then at the end, is when Jesus entirely removes darkness from the earth - including all who love it.

Again, according to scripture, this "Day of the Lord" begins the second half of the seven years of tribulation. Since that's the case, why is the first 3 ½ years also referred to as tribulation? For two reasons. One being because Daniel 9 refers to a final seven year period where sacrifices and offerings will be implemented in Jerusalem, but then will be cut off by the antichrist. So it's just that God, through Daniel, singled out a set of seven years. And then Jesus explained that before the Great Tribulation, before the entire "Day of the Lord" starts, that is, there will also be "the beginning of sorrows". So, we simply refer to this whole period as seven years.

Matthew 24 outlines what these are. But it stands to reason, if Daniel's prophecy says that in the middle of the seven years the antichrist will desecrate the temple, and that then the Great Tribulation, such has never been nor ever will be, will start, then the first half of this seven years must be 3 ½ years also. It's simple math. And since these first 3 ½ years have their own troubles with the rise of wars, persecution, famine, and natural disasters, it makes sense to refer to the entire seven year period as the seven year tribulations. Technically, we don't have to. We can just call it what the Bible says, which is Daniel's 70th, final week, wherein 3 ½ years of Great Tribulation transpire. But I personally prefer to call the entire week the seven year tribulation period. Regardless, I assure you, scripture does spell out a seven year period of troubles which transpires before Jesus comes to reign.

And I'd like to point something else out. People who don't understand the Bible and who God is, often deduce that He can't be a very loving God if He can allow evil into the world, or worse, allow eternal punishment for all evil-lovers who have zero capacity to repent. But as I mentioned earlier, the bottom line is that this is God's world. He can do whatever He wants.

Yet, the irony is He created man and free will, and then even gave them dominion, authority, and charge over the earth. And then stepped back and said everything is up to us - so long as we don't partake of the tree of knowledge of good and evil. Outside of this knowledge, earth life was glorious and perfect for humans, animals, and all the rest of creation. And we were also in perfect fellowship with the wondrous Creator.

But as you know, Adam and Eve did eat of that tree through the devil's deception, just as God knew they would do, which would be the beginning of their discovery of their infallibility, and the time granted for them to make their resolve for righteousness or evil, and also, to realize their need for the Majestic One to make them holy. And since Adam and Eve got that ball rolling, just about the full 6000 years have passed. Now it's time to bring creation and humanity into the seventh day of rest.

And, of course, God knew it would all go like this. He deliberately allowed it. Why? Because as I said earlier, free will was how God would let man determine for themselves what they wanted. Plus, He knew this is how we humans would discover that we aren't supreme. That we are capable of disregarding His majesty and doubting Him, despite all the amazing things He does. And not to mention that we are capable of disobedience and sin - which demonstrates the reality that we are dreadfully inferior beings to His Majesty. He had to allow us to discover how imperfect we are, because we aren't God, after all. And He had to allow us the freedom to choose if we, as individuals, prefer good... or evil.

In essence, all of mankind has the propensity for evil to one degree or another, and God knew that from day one. But, again, He had to let man discover this, and then demonstrate whether they are okay with it, or not. For those who hate their sin and evil tendencies, who wish they weren't so wretched, well, God made a way for them to be cleaned and made righteous - despite themselves. And He, being perfect and without sin, being HOLY, being all-powerful, accomplished this for us by reducing Himself to our level, and then allowing the ones He created, and through whom He chose to bring salvation to the world... to murder Him. He could have called legions of angels to smite them all. He could have flipped a supernatural switch and blew up the earth on the spot. But He ALLOWED the dust particles that He formed into humans and breathed breath into, to kill Him.

All for the purpose of bringing those same, wicked people, the opportunity to be forgiven for their sins, if they choose to repent and believe in the forgiveness He provides.

He accomplished this for us 2000 years ago. And everyone who had ever had genuine reverence for the one, true God, even prior to Christ's death and resurrection, qualified for the salvation provided at the Cross.

Understand that the Lord's death on the Cross provided a covenant between God and anyone who believed in the power of His blood to redeem them from their sin. This covenant fulfilled the first covenant God had made with Father Abraham which can be found in Genesis 12 through 15. In short, anyone who believed God and obeyed Him was in covenant with God, meaning, they belonged to God and He would take care of them. To the contrary, if they abandoned God by worshiping false gods or disobeying Him by sinning, and if they refused to repent after His lengthy, desperate warnings through His prophets, He would remove His hand of protection, and they'd suffer great punishments. And guess what always came of their discipline. If you said they finally repented and came back to God, you are right.

If you read the Old Testament, you see that this was the running theme. It happened over and over throughout the few thousand years before Jesus was born. Israel, the chosen nation, would be supernaturally blessed, win every war without explanation except that it was God, and their foes KNEW not to mess with them. But after years and years of goodness, they'd forget God and go off doing all sorts of evil things. Then God would speak warnings and messages through prophets like Jeremiah, Isaiah, Ezekiel, and more, to tell them, "Stop! Turn back to God before you suffer great discipline!". And they never listened despite their amazing, miraculous history with their loving Father. And sure enough, after decades of warnings, God would finally remove His hand of protection and they'd face great calamity, even being destroyed and taken captive at times.

Yet, a remnant would always come back to God because they knew He was the one true God.

After Jesus came, died and rose, providing an easier covenant where people don't have to offer sacrifices to be forgiven every year, most of Israel did not want to hear this. They were too locked in the religiosity and the power they'd acquired being the priests over the chosen nation. They didn't care about what really mattered - or God. That's why Jesus told them they were of their father the devil.

The point is that what Jesus did was fulfill the old, original covenant, by becoming the final sacrifice for all who believe. And this, then, was the new covenant. And this means that everyone who believes in Jesus as their Lord and Savior is grafted into the vine of Israel. This makes them "new covenant Israel". Even if they weren't born with any Jewish blood or in Israel, those who believe in Jesus are a royal priesthood, a holy nation according to Exodus 19:6 and 1 Peter 2:9. And for the past 2000 years, the truth of God's kingdom has been preached to all the world in order that all might be saved.

Now where I'm going with this is that for 2000 years the body of Christ has been growing. But there's a problem. Just as the Old Testament, old covenant Israel, continually abandoned their God, who preferred religiosity, rituals, traditions of man, regulations, and controlling people as well as using them for their personal gain, the new covenant Israel, the Christian church, has been doing the same thing! And today, we're worse than ever. The church looks just like the world. We have a form of godliness but deny the power thereof (2 Timothy 3:5). The Bible says not to love the world. But the church totally disregards this. The church is full of self, idolatry, lust, sin, etc. And the sad part is, they think they are safe just because they are Christian. Many churches teach that God's grace is sufficient, that if you sin, it's okay. His grace covers you. You are automatically forgiven. But it's all lies. You have to literally respond to the conviction of the Holy Spirit and turn from sin. The power of Christ is in us to help us to overcome sin, addiction, and all else. But we aren't taught this. We think saying we're Christians and attending church on occasion means we have "get out of Hell free" cards. And it's all wrong.

Meanwhile, here we are... Jesus is ready to come back to reign on earth as King! He could have stayed and taken over 2000 years ago. But it wasn't time.

The seven days of creation in Genesis is an outline, or illustration, of the first seven thousand years of earth life - and God rested on day seven. The sixth day is just about to end and is why Jesus is coming back at the end of the seven year tribulation. He comes to reign for the seventh thousand years - the day of rest. Because He is the Sabbath Rest. Well, if all the math of the scholars is correct, then this means the seventh day begins... in 2030, or pretty close to it! Which is why it is strongly suspected that the seven year tribulation must begin either in 2023, or very soon after!

But the problem is if Jesus came back right now, MOST PEOPLE WILL NOT HAVE BEEN CLEANSED OF THEIR INIQUITY AND MADE CAPABLE OF RECEIVING THEIR GLORIFIED BODIES! They wouldn't be able to escape the Great Tribulation because people's spirits aren't capable of connecting with their glorified bodies unless they're purified by the blood of Jesus! This requires LEGITIMATE repentance to happen.

As I said, even the Christian church is not in right standing and pure. Yes, they believe Jesus is God in the flesh and that His blood atones for sin. But they don't remain in Him and the cleansing power of His blood. They don't know Him. They don't truly worship Him. They still serve themselves, the world, sin, and mammon! Many are living in sin and think it's okay. They have a place for God in their lives, but disregard His heart and precepts daily. It's like being in a marriage where both spouses officially remain in the marriage, but they have little to no regard for one another. They put themselves first above their other half. And sadly, many others don't even realize they are in sin! Because sin has become an okay thing! What's good is now called evil, and evil is now considered to be good, just like it says in Isaiah 5:20! Some kind of do know they're in sin, and they kind of repent, but ultimately don't care enough to seek God and discover the power of Christ and the Spirit in them to overcome sin. --So they remain in allegiance with the dark kingdom to one degree or another.

Jesus, God in the flesh, does not want to come back until all who belong to Him are made right by His blood. But almost nobody cares about this because the world and even believers are so entitled, full of pride and self, and idolatry, that they can't hear God beckoning them to turn from their iniquity and truly come back to Him. Which means, if He did come now, billions that belong to Him would not be right and could not be reconciled to the Father... If Jesus tried to give an unclean person their glorified body, **it would vaporize them!**

This is why He has no choice but to crack the whip and get everyone's attention! It is precisely the reason God had to dedicate a final seven year period of tumultuous troubles... to bring people back to a place of reverence for an Almighty, Majestic God, to snap them back into reality and to strip His people of their idols, of their self sufficiency, pride, spirits of entitlement, their out-of-control flesh, their lusts, and even their unbelief; humbling them all, because they had refused to humble themselves... so that all who are His... will finally repent and be purified.

Chapter Eight
What to Do & How to Be Safe

You likely know what I'm about to say, which is that your only hope and refuge is to repent and be truly right with God. This is how we hide in Christ. But what exactly does this look like?

Putting it simply, anyone who believes that Jesus is God in the flesh and that He came to die for the sin of the world, who also knows they are sinners in need of the supernatural cleansing power of the righteous blood of Jesus, can repent, call on the Name of Jesus, and be saved.

But it doesn't stop there. The Bible tells us to work out our salvation with fear and trembling. This means you want to remain in a healthy fear of His Majesty, remaining forever aware that apart from Him, you are filthy, and that you need His Spirit and power daily to help you overcome your sin nature. So, it's all about posture. You must remain humble and dependent on the power of Christ in you to overcome sin. This requires daily communication with and acknowledgment of Him.

Next, sanctification comes by renewing your mind with the Word of God. Prior to Christ, your mind was filled with, and dominated by, darkness. So, you have to daily give your mind to Christ by clothing it with His truth. This will supernaturally force everything false inside of your mind, heart, and soul, to expel. As you press into the Word by the power of the Holy Spirit, you will be transformed. You will see your sin and wickedness lose power more and more. You will experience greater and greater victory over sin, and will have more and more fruits of the Holy Spirit, which are found in Galatians 5.

In addition to all this, you want to thank God daily, all day, for everything. Even troubles. He says to count it all as joy. And you want to worship Him; show Him great honor and praise Him. These connect your spirit with His Spirit, which end up empowering you. And you'll begin feeling the wonder of His presence and goodness more and more.

As for what not to do, ask God what He wants to clean up first. He's very gentle and patient. Not that He'll let things slide very long, but He understands that His power in you is a work of glory in process. But find out what you're doing that must be stopped right away, and then use the power of Christ to stop. Trust me when I tell you - you cannot stop the sins personally. Some people have a bit of will power, but most people do not. It takes Christ's power to stop the sins. So you say,

"God, I want to stop this sin, I renounce this behavior. It's an offense to You and Your kingdom and I want to walk right before You. But I can't stop this sin myself, I do not have the power in and of myself. But I do have YOUR power in me, Jesus! So, though I cannot overcome this, You can help me overcome it by YOUR Spirit in me. I desperately need Your help, Lord. And I trust Your power is capable. I yield to You, Lord. I call on Your power, in this, Father. As I face the temptation, help me to call on Your power and resist it in the Name of Jesus. Because I want to be obedient to You, Lord. In Jesus' Name, Amen."

Now, sometimes you'll do this, but other times you'll neglect to obey God by yielding to Him and calling on His power to overcome. You will need to repent as quickly as possible and return to your resolve to obey from that moment forward. Yes, you'll slip from time to time. But always get back up on the horse of obedience and REPENT as soon as possible. And don't purposely sin thinking you'll just repent, because that's not a heart that truly longs to obey God, and He knows it. Such repentance isn't really repentance, and God knows it. The blood doesn't apply in such cases. No, you truly want to pursue righteousness.

When you do genuinely slip up and sin, don't spend a day or week or month feeling sorry for yourself or guilty. We all fall short. That's why we need the blood of Jesus in the first place. Just get back in line as quickly as possible, study the Word, and have honest communication or prayers with the Lord.

If you're living like this, then you are abiding in Christ and this puts a covering over you, like the shadow of the Almighty found in Psalm 91. So this is where you want to be. Genuinely pursuing God and His righteousness with all your heart - and quickly repenting when you mess up. That's it!

I'm telling you, it's urgent that you get on the straight and narrow right away! You need to get close to God so that you can discern the lies and deceptions of darkness, and so that you can be safe in light of all the terrible things that are beginning to happen all around us, everywhere! Satan is desperate to muddle up, or even destroy believers because we are what's interfering with his measure of success in his takeover. But he cannot touch people who are living a life yielded to God and pursuing righteousness. So we must fix our eyes on God and not mess around anymore. There's no more time for games or foolishness. Those who aren't hiding in the shadow of the Almighty will suffer in any number of ways, to one degree or another!

If you doubt that what I'm telling you is spot on, just watch. If famine becomes a major problem starting in 2025 or sooner, that's a HUGE indicator that the Great Tribulation will begin in 2027 (or 2028, depending on the timing of the covenant with many). And mark my word, the famine I'm speaking of will be catastrophic, taking the lives of **hundreds of millions of people**! There will be a drastic increase in the occurrences of supernatural phenomena, including angel visitations, lying signs and wonders, and miraculous glory revivals in various parts of the world. And in a few years from now, laws will be made against true followers of Christ to stop preaching against the lies and apostasy and all else. And at some point over the next few years, there will be a major earthquake in the USA that will occur back-to-back with Israel's two-state solution agreement. And finally, after all this, an asteroid will hit the earth and some kind of plague will hit those who don't have the seal of God on their foreheads (see Rev. 9:4). If you don't believe me now, I beg of you to believe me as these things unfold, otherwise you'll suffer greatly. The last moments to repent and get sincerely right with God are upon us! Whoever doesn't will BE LEFT BEHIND FOR THE HORRORS OF THE GREAT TRIBULATION! I don't want this for you!

So I close this letter asking you to please, please pray about all this... and get right with God a.s.a.p.

Love, Mom

www.ingramcontent.com/pod-product-compliance
Lightning Source LLC
Chambersburg PA
CBHW070854050426
42453CB00012B/2200